Get Their Recipe NOW

DISCOVER THE LEGACY OF YOUR LOVED ONES

Greg Jenkins

Get Their Recipe Now
Discover the Legacy of Your Loved Ones
Copyright © 2018 Gregory L. Jenkins
All rights reserved worldwide

Cover photo by Gregory L. Jenkins
Cover design by Gregory L. Jenkins and Linda Bonney Olin
Copyright ©2018 Gregory L. Jenkins

Published by Gregory L. Jenkins
New York USA
www.gregsentertainment.com

ISBN-13: 978-0-9975367-6-8
ISBN-10: 0997536764

CONTENTS

For my mom.
May 26, 1930 – September 25, 2018
How I wish I could have just one more great conversation with you.

For my sons.
So you will have this after I have gone home.

ACKNOWLEDGMENTS

There is one person who without I could not have completed this work, that one is my wife, Joanna. She believed in me when I did not. She is a blessing every day and I thank her for her love and support.

Many thanks to my in-laws, Ma and Pa Baker. They never knew when a chapter was going to hit their inbox, but they were always glad to look it over and give me feedback.

I also must thank my friend Linda Bonney Olin for seeing me through the arduous journey of formatting this book and designing the cover with me. Her patience is beyond compare.

Introduction

At this very moment, my mother sits in an Alzheimer's unit, her mind sharp as a tack one minute then lost in fear and forgetfulness the next. For this reason I will never again have my favorite birthday cake. I realize that sounds childish for a man in his fifties, but I cannot help lament the loss of that confection from my youth, just as you might long to once again enjoy a favorite song, saying, inside joke, or meal that was a cherished part of your past.

Through this writing I hope to encourage others to avoid the pitfall that has led me to a place where I can only dream of a recipe that is lost forever in the mind of a woman who cared for me my entire life. The pitfall I refer to is ignorance of the important equation between time and priority.

Within the pages that follow are keys to finding out who parents, guardians, or other beloved elders in your life truly are. Some of these keys you may already know well, and others you may not have even considered inquiring about. If you take some time with each chapter and seek the answers to what is asked, you will take a wonderful journey of discovery into their inner being ... and even uncover ingredients into the recipe of yourself.

There are several ways you can use this book. It can serve as a guide for discussion. Or give it to someone to fill in their responses and return it to you. Perhaps you will fill in the blanks yourself and pass it on to your children so they can hold a piece of you forever.

Although I have provided space after each question for answers to be written right here in the book, some answers may require more room than this book offers. Rather than limit the responses, I suggest using an additional notebook or journal as needed.

Regardless of how you move forward, I hope you will be motivated to open the conversations suggested in this book with every significant person in your life.

These days, everyone is busy. But as I look back on my life, I can clearly see how the focus of my attention has wasted away many hours that can never be regained. Time is a commodity that I, and many others, have squandered in this fast-paced, moment-to-moment life we lead. I urge you not to let the pressures of today's commitments prevent you from taking a wonderful journey to the past with your loved ones ... while there's still time.

This Book Is About the Life of:

Name: _____

Maiden name: _____

Other names used:

_____

Born on: _____/_____/_____

Born to mother:

_____

Born to father:

_____

Place of birth:

_____

Maternal grandparents:

_____

Paternal grandparents:

_____

Siblings (names and number of years older or younger):

_____

_____

_____

Other significant family members:

_____

_____

_____

The Speed of Life

It is easy to get wrapped up in life's frantic pace. Work responsibilities, school events, and community commitments can fill our calendars to the point where these activities consume every day and take our eyes off of the truly important things in life. Our hectic schedules steal from us the most basic opportunities for human interaction, such as the evening meal, Sunday church, or having one day a week when family time is the focus.

Years come and go so fast. Seasons and events become a blur. "Can you believe it's the holidays again?" "How can it be your birthday already?" As we get older, time seems to accelerate. Yet we do so little to preserve it.

Even though the finite tenure we have on this planet is out of our control, we do have the power to decide how that time is spent. If your family's schedule is taken up with every activity offered at your children's school and you find yourself constantly on the run to keep up, you can make the choice to trim that schedule. Community involvement, work schedules, and school activities are all essential, but moderation is the key. When was the last time you sat and just talked with your kids, spouse, mom, or dad, with no outside influence involved? If it has been more than a week, perhaps you need to eliminate one or more of the factors that interfere with your fleeting opportunities to connect with the people who really matter to you.

Our time on earth is limited. None of us knows when our last day of physical life or mental awareness will be. This is why the topics in this book are discussed with a sense of urgency. We must make the most of the time we are given, to ensure that we receive as much knowledge as we can about our heritage and to share as much about ourselves as we can with those who follow.

This requires a concerted effort on your part, to take hold of time and structure it for what you know to be the priorities. This is a call to action. It will not happen on its own. There truly is no time to waste!

Use the following template to create your plan of action. By writing down steps, and dates to complete them, you may find it easier to ensure that you have what you need from your loved ones and give to your loved ones what they need.

My Plan

I will start working through this book on (date): _____/_____/_____

I hope to have it finished by (date): _____/_____/_____

I will take this step:

_____

On this date: _____/_____/_____

I will take this step:

_____

On this date: _____/_____/_____

I will take this step:

_____

On this date: _____/_____/_____

I will take this step:

_____

On this date: _____/_____/_____

I will take this step:

_____

On this date: _____/_____/_____

I will take this step:

_____

On this date: _____/_____/_____

I will take this step:

_____

On this date: _____ / _____ / _____

I will take this step:

_____

On this date: _____ / _____ / _____

I will take this step:

_____

On this date: _____ / _____ / _____

I will take this step:

_____

On this date: _____ / _____ / _____

I will take this step:

_____

On this date: _____ / _____ / _____

I will take this step:

_____

On this date: _____ / _____ / _____

I will take this step:

_____

On this date: _____ / _____ / _____

I will take this step:

_____

On this date: _____ / _____ / _____

I will take this step:

_____

On this date: _____/_____/_____

I will take this step:

_____

On this date: _____/_____/_____

I will take this step:

_____

On this date: _____/_____/_____

I will take this step:

_____

On this date: _____/_____/_____

I will take this step:

_____

On this date: _____/_____/_____

I will take this step:

_____

On this date: _____/_____/_____

I will take this step:

_____

On this date: _____/_____/_____

I will take this step:

_____

On this date: _____/_____/_____

Get Started

For many the most difficult part of a journey like this is getting started. If you feel compelled to work through this book wholly, or in part, but are having a hard time knowing where to start, here is a short list of questions you can begin with. This may serve to break the ice with loved ones who might be reluctant to dive into a series of lengthy discussions. It could also help you feel more comfortable about asking deeper questions if you launch the project with these simple ones.

Even though these questions seem pretty basic, don't be afraid to let conversation develop about each answer. There may be an anecdote with each response that you surely do not want to miss.

Taking notes and writing things down, either in the space provided in this book or another notebook will minimize the revisions we are all subject to make in our minds and keep the stories as fresh and accurate as possible.

Quick Questions to Get the Ball Rolling

What is your favorite color?

_____

What is your lucky/favorite number?

_____

What is your favorite flower?

_____

What is your favorite Holiday?

_____

What is your favorite season of year?

_____

How old were you when you had your first kiss?

_____

What was your favorite vacation?

_____

What was your first car?

_____

What was your favorite car?

_____

What is your favorite animal?

_____

What was your favorite pet?

_____

Who was your best friend growing up?

_____

What is your favorite candy?

_____

What is your favorite ice cream?

_____

What is your favorite cake?

_____

What is your favorite pie?

_____

What is your favorite cookie?

_____

What is your favorite meal?

_____

Coffee or tea?

_____

What is your favorite drink?

_____

Do you or did you ever play a musical instrument?

_____

EXTRA NOTES:

_____

_____

_____

_____

_____

_____

_____

_____

Get It in Writing

When discussing the theme of this book with a friend one day, she told me she wished she had anything that was handwritten by her father. Now in her seventies, she has no cards, letters, not so much as a note penned by him. If any ever existed, they had been thrown out with the trash, seemingly insignificant.

Do you have anything handwritten by your parents or another elder you hold in high regard? Letters, notes, recipes, even a jotted grocery list can put you in touch with them after they are gone. They touched that paper, put pen or pencil to it, and even if for the briefest moment, it was their focus. Handwriting is as individual as fingerprints and unique to each person. There are few things in life that are so personal.

If you look around, you may discover pages you never realized existed. You may find letters written before you were born. Perhaps you will discover a note scribbled hurriedly as your loved one huddled in a foxhole in time of war. These treasures have a value greater than gold. You can pull them out anytime you want to experience a piece of those you cherish.

If you have nothing handwritten by your loved ones, ask for a simple card or a funny note. Urge them to write down anything they want you to know. Or give them this book and ask them to write notes in it.

It is equally important to write something for the ones you love. Send each of your children a note in your handwriting. Tell them how you feel about them and about yourself. Fill in your own answers to the questions in this book and gift it to your children. Give them insight into who you are. Ask them to keep your writings safe because you know the day will come when they will be glad they have them to hold on to.

We are all busy people, living in a world of e-mails and text messages. Communication has become impersonal. But if you make an effort to put pen to paper, then a personal piece of you will live on. And if you ask those you revere to write something to you, there will be a permanent part of them that you can hold onto and pass down through generations.

Write It Down Now

I have something handwritten from:

_____

Written to:_____

Dated: _____/_____/_____

The note is stored at:

_____

Topic:

_____

Notes:

_____

_____

I have something handwritten from:

_____

Written to: _____

Dated: _____/_____/_____

The note is stored at:

_____

Topic:

_____

Notes:

_____

_____

I have something handwritten from:

_____

Written to: : _____

Dated: _____/_____/_____

The note is stored at:

_____

Topic:

_____

Notes:

_____

_____

_____

I have something handwritten from:

_____

Written to: _____

Dated: _____/_____/_____

The note is stored at:

_____

Topic:

_____

Notes:

_____

_____

_____

The Places You Lived

The neighborhood or neighborhoods we grow up in, as well as where we spend our adult years, influence our attitudes and behaviors. This stands true for your elders as well.

Some people live their entire lives in one community. They were born, raised and worked within the same circle and their roots run deep there. The houses they live in may be the ones they were born in.

Other people live in multiple communities within their lifetimes. For instance, children in military families move frequently while growing up. And many young adults move away for education and work opportunities. Each home where someone lives is unique. Every house or apartment is different from the one before. The streets, while possibly similar to others, exhibit distinct nuances. The local stores and markets may be characterized by region or ethnicity. These details can be quite enjoyable to recall and note with your loved one.

Involvement in one's community is another factor to take note of. Was your mom or dad involved heavily in community functions? Perhaps Grandpa was a volunteer fireman. Did Grandma spend a lot of time working with the local historical society or was she a member of a community service or faith organization, helping those in need? Then there are those who simply kept to themselves, tending to their own daily routines. Regardless, community involvement is a significant element of who your loved ones were and are.

There are many chapters to the lives of those we love. Where they lived and the surroundings they lived within are keys to understanding a great deal about them and, in turn, ourselves. Enjoy this discussion with them. As they describe the surroundings they enjoyed, or endured, try to picture them there. Let them relive what they want to and put on paper what they can. This is their history.

Where You Have Lived

Address:

_____

Community involvement:

_____

_____

_____

Stores and markets:

_____

_____

Restaurants and eateries:

_____

_____

Friends:

_____

_____

Special memories:

_____

_____

_____

_____

_____

_____

Address:

_____

Community involvement:

_____

_____

_____

Stores and markets:

_____

_____

Restaurants and eateries:

_____

_____

Friends:

_____

_____

Special memories:

_____

_____

_____

_____

_____

_____

_____

_____

_____

Address:

_____

Community involvement:

_____

_____

_____

Stores and markets:

_____

_____

Restaurants and eateries:

_____

_____

Friends:

_____

_____

Special memories:

_____

_____

_____

_____

_____

_____

_____

_____

_____

Address:

_____

Community involvement:

_____

_____

_____

Stores and markets:

_____

_____

Restaurants and eateries:

_____

_____

Friends:

_____

_____

Special memories:

_____

_____

_____

_____

_____

_____

_____

_____

_____

Address:

_____

Community involvement:

_____

_____

_____

Stores and markets:

_____

_____

Restaurants and eateries:

_____

_____

Friends:

_____

_____

Special memories:

_____

_____

_____

_____

_____

_____

_____

_____

_____

Address:

_____

Community involvement:

_____

_____

_____

Stores and markets:

_____

_____

_____

Restaurants and eateries:

_____

_____

_____

Friends:

_____

_____

Special memories:

_____

_____

_____

_____

_____

_____

_____

_____

_____

School

From the moment we are born, we begin to learn about the world around us. We grow to take our place in our family structure. But outside the confines of our own home, schools have a tremendous impact upon who we become.

From grammar school through high school and beyond, most people follow a common path of formal education. However, every child is unique in how and what they learn. Students tend to gravitate to some subjects more than others. While one student excels at math or history, another might blossom in the arts or sciences.

It is not uncommon to have differences in strengths and weaknesses within a family. One sibling may be a hands-on learner and advance in the trade fields, such as carpentry or plumbing. Others may be inclined to learn through reading classical literature. Some may prove to be proficient at both. The possibilities are as many as there are individuals.

Perhaps the most influential aspects of schools are teachers. They dominate our developmental years, not just in the subjects they expound, but in the behaviors they exhibit. Almost without exception a teacher, or teachers, have had a memorable impact on our lives.

Socialization is another important facet of the school experience. Meeting others who have different backgrounds can be powerful factors in someone's development. The different ethnicities and religious beliefs that students are exposed to may open their eyes to a world that is much larger and more varied than they are accustomed to.

The school activities we participate in can tell a great deal about who we are. Perhaps playing an instrument in a marching band is one person's focus. Being on a football or baseball team might be the desire of another individual and yet someone else may want to spend their time in an art club or working on the school newspaper. These activities allow a more personal nature to shine given that they are chosen rather than assigned as part of a school curriculum.

Through all their school involvement, it is likely that your elders developed friendships. Some of these friendships may have begun in kindergarten and lasted throughout the entire school experience and beyond while others came and went with the changing of classes and maturity. Many friends may have taken part in the same activities as your loved ones. It is important to note these friendships because they are a part of those we care about.

The path your loved ones took during their school years cannot be categorized in just a kindergarten through twelfth grade structure. There is much more to those years than can be put within those book ends. Go into this with an open mind. You may be surprised at some of the stories you hear. When they share their experience with you try to recall your own school experience and compare their story to your own. You will likely see a great deal of similarities and enjoy just as many differences.

What Schools Did you Attend

Kindergarten/Teachers:

_____

_____

Friends:

_____

Activities/Memories:

_____

First Grade/Teachers:

_____

_____

Friends:

_____

Activities/Memories:

_____

Second Grade/Teachers:

_____

_____

Friends:

_____

_____

Activities/Memories:

_____

_____

Third Grade/Teachers:

_____

_____

Friends:

_____

_____

Activities/Memories:

_____

_____

Fourth Grade/Teachers:

_____

_____

Friends:

_____

_____

Activities/Memories:

_____

_____

Fifth Grade/Teachers:

_____

_____

Friends:

_____

_____

Activities/Memories:

_____

_____

Sixth Grade/Teachers:

_____

_____

_____

Friends:

_____

_____

_____

Activities/Memories:

_____

_____

_____

_____

_____

Seventh Grade/Teachers:

_____

_____

_____

Friends:

_____

_____

_____

Activities/Memories:

_____

_____

_____

_____

_____

Eighth Grade/Teachers:

_____

_____

_____

Friends:

_____

_____

_____

Activities/Memories:

_____

_____

_____

_____

_____

Ninth Grade/Teachers:

_____

_____

_____

Friends:

_____

_____

_____

Activities/Memories:

_____

_____

_____

_____

Tenth Grade/Teachers:

_____

_____

_____

Friends:

_____

_____

_____

Activities/Memories:

_____

_____

_____

_____

_____

Eleventh Grade/Teachers:

_____

_____

_____

Friends:

_____

_____

_____

Activities/Memories:

_____

_____

_____

_____

_____

Twelfth Grade/Teachers:

_____

_____

_____

Friends:

_____

_____

_____

Activities/Memories:

_____

_____

_____

_____

_____

Post High School/Trade School/College/Military:

_____

_____

_____

Friends:

_____

_____

_____

Activities/Memories:

_____

_____

_____

_____

_____

Who They Were Before You

Just as you have had iconic phases in your life, your loved ones have had their own patches of time that hold tremendous significance. It can be difficult to imagine your parents, grandparents, or other elderly people in your life as anyone other than the people you have seen every day for as long as you can remember. You have witnessed these individuals going to work, paying the bills, cooking your meals, being involved in church and community. From your limited perspective this is who they are, always have been, and always will be. To think of them in any other capacity is challenging.

However, before you came along, their lives were very different. Wouldn't you love to find out who they were before you?

There are a few significant pieces of their past that could help you put this puzzle together.

Music is a universal language. Have you ever heard a song that triggered a memory of something in your youth? Like being in a time machine, you were transported back to a particular moment in your history. You remember who you were with, where you were, what you were doing, even what you were eating. The effect of music on our loved ones is no different. Though their style of music may seem antiquated, it is as heartfelt and meaningful to them as any song you cherish.

Your grandmother may not verbalize it, but when she hears a particular song, in her mind she is dancing in a club, barn, or school that you will probably never see. She may reminisce of her wedding day and that special song she danced to with her new husband. When she relates to you the music she enjoyed, you may find out that Granny was quite the rabble-rouser or that she was very involved in church socials. Whether she was a flapper, a jitter-bugger, or a choir member, this is a part of who she was and an important piece to the puzzle of who she is now.

Movies often mark some iconic moments in history. Blockbusters of a bygone era can stand as fresh in the memory of our parents or guardians as if the film were just released. These movies might have a meaning of some depth or simply provide recollections of a positive, carefree moment in time. Movie stars that they idolized for their beauty, charisma, or persona stand out as nuggets from their past. Genres such as horror, comedy, drama, or musicals might be favorites of your loved ones. Opening this topic could elicit reminiscence of specific theaters in their town or groups of friends going to the movies together.

Radio and television programs that affected our elders can be a window into who they were before you existed. Whether your parents' favorite programs were *Fibber McGee and Molly*, *I Love Lucy*, or *The Lone Ranger*, you may want to know what characters they related to or despised, and why. The profound effect from radio or television may not be the shows themselves so much as where and with whom your folks enjoyed them. Did the family gather around the radio or television at a specific time each week? Was there a great deal of anticipation to share that time and enjoy that show together? For many, these were important events on the timeline of their youth.

Literature is another medium that may shed some light upon who your loved ones were before you came along. Did they prefer romances, westerns, or whimsical fiction? Were history books or science magazines their preferred fare? If they took the time to read a book, or a series of books of a certain genre or topic, this was a predominant part of their makeup.

One of the benefits of the time we live in is the technology we have at our disposal. When you ask questions such as "What was your favorite song?" or "Did you have a favorite program?" look for their answers on the internet. Old-time radio shows, television programs, recordings, books, and movies are readily available, many for free. Travel back with your loved ones and relive the time and events that mean so much to them. These portals into their past will make this segment of discovery richer than you can imagine.

Who You Were Before Me

What music was important to you and why?

_____

_____

_____

_____

_____

_____

What were your favorite movies, actors, or theater-related memories?

_____

_____

_____

_____

_____

_____

Were there any special radio or television programs you enjoyed? Whom did you enjoy them with?

_____

_____

_____

_____

_____

_____

_____

Did you have any favorite books, authors, or literary genres?

_____

_____

_____

_____

_____

_____

_____

_____

EXTRA NOTES:

_____

_____

_____

_____

_____

_____

_____

_____

_____

_____

_____

_____

_____

_____

_____

Jobs

The way an individual earns money may take on many forms over a lifetime. Jobs change with age, availability, and need.

When we are young our employment options may be limited, but opportunities do exist. Mowing lawns, babysitting, raking leaves, or shoveling snow are all jobs that we can do at a fairly young age. As we get older those tasks remain, but more possibilities open for us. Bagging groceries at the market, being a lifeguard or a groundskeeper at a park are a few of many jobs that teenagers can do to make money.

Many factors influence the jobs we choose as adults. Are we going to take on the family farm or business? Will our education determine our professional direction? Military experience might give us a marketable skill for civilian life or be a career itself. Sometimes, after starting on a course we believe to be the only way, our hearts and desires change, so, we choose a different way to earn a living. At other times we are forced into career changes due to economic circumstances such as business closures or layoffs resulting in job loss.

Understanding the motivation behind taking a specific job can help you better know your loved ones. Was there a passion for the work chosen or was this the only work available at the time? Perhaps there was an expectation that an individual would follow in the family footsteps? Beyond those reasons there are financial motivations. A youth may have taken a job just for spending money, or in difficult times, to help support the family. Learning why your loved ones performed the jobs they had can provide tremendous insight into their character.

Most people have held at least one, if not several, jobs over their lifetime. These are significant pieces of who they were and who they have become. The people you know have been shaped in many ways by the work they performed throughout their lives. Their experiences from these jobs are a part of who they are today and you can understand them better by knowing what they have worked at and why.

Jobs

Where was your first job and what did you do there?

_____

How old were you?

_____

Why did you take it?

_____

Did you like it? Why?

_____

_____

Why did you leave?

_____

Where was another job and what did you do there?

_____

How old were you?

_____

Why did you take it?

_____

Did you like it? Why?

_____

_____

Why did you leave?

_____

Where was another job and what did you do there?

_____

How old were you?

_____

Why did you take it?

_____

Did you like it? Why?

_____

_____

Why did you leave?

_____

_____

Where was another job and what did you do there?

_____

How old were you?

_____

Why did you take it?

_____

Did you like it? Why?

_____

_____

Why did you leave?

_____

_____

Where was another job and what did you do there?

_____

How old were you?

_____

Why did you take it?

_____

Did you like it? Why?

_____

_____

Why did you leave?

_____

_____

Where was another job and what did you do there?

_____

How old were you?

_____

Why did you take it?

_____

Did you like it? Why?

_____

_____

Why did you leave?

_____

_____

Where was another job and what did you do there?

_____

How old were you?

_____

Why did you take it?

_____

Did you like it? Why?

_____

_____

Why did you leave?

_____

_____

Where was another job and what did you do there?

_____

How old were you?

_____

Why did you take it?

_____

Did you like it? Why?

_____

_____

Why did you leave?

_____

_____

Where was another job and what did you do there?

_____

How old were you?

_____

Why did you take it?

_____

Did you like it? Why?

_____

_____

Why did you leave?

_____

_____

Where was another job and what did you do there?

_____

How old were you?

_____

Why did you take it?

_____

Did you like it? Why?

_____

_____

Why did you leave?

_____

_____

Hobbies

Building car models, fishing, gardening, and woodworking are just a few of the hobbies that people all over the world enjoy. As they grow, children gravitate toward hobbies related to their personalities and aptitudes.

No doubt your parents or guardians had activities that piqued their interest. For some, their hobbies were introduced to them by elders in their lives. In other cases the idea may have come to them from some source outside the family. Or the impetus of a hobby might have been their imagination. Regardless of the origin, these interests helped develop skills that affected the path they followed later in life. Many people carry their hobbies into adulthood.

Perhaps you have witnessed, or even participated in, the hobbies of your elderly loved ones. You might have quilted with your mother, learned crocheting from Grandma, assembled a ham radio with Gramps, or run a model train with your dad. Have you gone camping, hiking, or hunting with a loved one, enjoying nature's beauty? If so, you have shared this important part of them and let it become a part of who you are.

Even so, there is an important question to make certain you ask while there is still time. That question is *Why.* Why do they enjoy these activities? As you hear tales of how these interests developed, you may learn that their passion was born of a book they read or a dream they had.

In some instances the hobby is no longer present but you can see the result of that early learning experience in the profession your loved ones chose. It is possible their vocations stemmed from the activities enjoyed as a child. The hobbies they participated in were practice, a way of perfecting their craft.

Not everyone has had the chance to follow their passions. For many, beloved childhood activities were outgrown or cast aside. Pressure from parents, relatives, teachers, or peers may have caused them to abandon their interests for more mainstream, profitable endeavors. The business of living could have gotten in the way of their enjoyable pastimes.

When you broach the topic of the hobbies your elders enjoyed, or still enjoy, you will be opening a door for them to relive happy, creative times in their lives. For those who are no longer active in their hobbies, this discussion might rekindle a flame, causing them to pursue it once more. What an opportunity that would be for you both to share in making memories together!

What Are or Were Your Hobbies?

Hobby #1:

_____

How did you get involved in this hobby?

_____

_____

_____

_____

What did you find most enjoyable about this hobby?

_____

_____

_____

_____

Hobby #2:

_____

How did you get involved in this hobby?

_____

_____

_____

What did you find most enjoyable about this hobby?

_____

_____

_____

_____

Hobby #3:

_____

How did you get involved in this hobby?

_____

_____

_____

_____

What did you find most enjoyable about this hobby?

_____

_____

_____

_____

_____

Hobby #4:

_____

How did you get involved in this hobby?

_____

_____

_____

_____

What did you find most enjoyable about this hobby?

_____

_____

_____

_____

_____

Hopes and Dreams

Before your cherished elders became Mom or Dad, Grandma or Grandpa, they had hopes and dreams. Talents and gifts they fully intended to use to better themselves and their families may have been put aside in order to get down to the reality of life. Did your father want to be a fireman or a doctor? Was a baseball career in Grandpa's future, or did he plan to rank high in the military? Was Mom going to travel the world helping others, or own a grocery store to serve the people of her community?

Life rarely takes the course we set for it. Whether it is destiny or simply the variables of survival, our paths often deviate from the aspirations of our youth. Some people are able to stay the course of their chosen career, but even they may have hopes that never came to pass.

For many, the journey to their dreams has been altered by unforeseen occurrences. Some are as subtle as the lack of opportunity to bring a goal to fruition, resulting in the acceptance of a more mundane existence. Other circumstances may be as drastic as war or the unexpected loss of a loved one. Regardless, there still exists a part within our loved ones that holds to those dreams of yesteryear.

The questions we need to ask seem simple. "What did you want to be?" "What did you want to do with your life?" We might even ask, "What stopped you?" The answers to these questions might not be easy for them to share. They might feel that their youthful musings are now unwarranted aspirations that have no validity. Or that these are secrets best left inside because they are too painful to verbalize. Your loved ones may not want to share their unrecognized hopes because they don't want you to feel as if your existence was a barrier.

Respect the level of sharing they wish to provide. Pressing them will only lead to angst and may end your discovery. However, with compassion, patience, understanding, and earnest, uncondemning interest, you may smile together as you both explore this important part of who they are.

Take your time recording the hopes and dreams of those you care about. You may not get all the answers you hope for, but enjoy the responses you receive.

What Were Your Hopes and Dreams?

When you were young, what did you want to be as an adult?

_____

_____

_____

Why did you want to become this person?

_____

_____

_____

_____

_____

Do you feel you achieved some measure of success in your goal? If so how?

_____

_____

_____

_____

If not, what do you believe stopped you?

_____

_____

_____

_____

_____

_____

_____

_____

Keepsakes

Heirlooms, trinkets, and souvenirs adorn most households. Items set upon shelves depict memories, interests, and history of individuals and their families.

A handmade clay ashtray may sit on Grandma's kitchen counter. A fishing rod over Grandpa's fireplace or perhaps a collection of old thimbles in Mom's sewing room might be things that caught your eye over the years. The types of keepsakes are almost endless. Although these pieces of memorabilia might not seem important to you, they hold tremendous meaning to those you love.

Some of the items that decorate the homes of your elders were handed down for generations. Certain pieces may bear a high monetary value, but often the sentimental value is far greater. For example, buttons from a civil war jacket worn by a great grandfather could bring a high price at auction but are priceless within a family. For these types of heirlooms it is critical to get the history, including any documentation supporting their past. This will ensure that their story is preserved for generations to come.

Many possessions cherished by people are of a far more personal nature. When a child creates a gift for a parent or grandparent and presents it to them with pride and love, the value of that item becomes etched on the heart of the recipient. A ragged pot holder, now stained and worn, might be the most prized possession of Mom. The handmade wooden clock on Dad's wall could bring warmth to him every time he looks at it. These treasures of the heart are irreplaceable and should be preserved.

Whether you recognize the value your loved ones placed on their belongings is irrelevant. The fact is that they found joy in having these items near. To have the chance to learn what these bits of their lives are, and why they cherished them, is itself a treasure. By logging as much history as you can you ensure that those who come after will enjoy these pieces too.

Keepsakes

Item:

_____

Origin:

_____

Significance:

_____

_____

Item:

_____

Origin:

_____

Significance:

_____

_____

Item:

_____

Origin:

_____

Significance:

_____

_____

Item:

_____

Origin:

_____

Significance:

_____

_____

Item:

_____

Origin:

_____

Significance:

_____

_____

Item:

_____

Origin:

_____

Significance:

_____

_____

Notes:

_____

_____

Success and Failure

We have all attempted various things during our lives. Some went well while others did not. Business ventures, athletic aspirations, building projects, or personal goals may have been successful or fallen into failure. These experiences are building blocks of our character. We would not be who we are today if not for events in our lives that taught us our strengths and weaknesses—and more important, how to deal with them.

The memory of those trials and triumphs live within the minds and hearts of your loved ones. Some may elicit a smile while others may cause a cringe.

Herein lies an opportunity to get to know the very foundation of someone you have had a one-sided understanding of your entire life. This conversation will show you the core of their existence and how they became who they are today. You may find some root causes for why you feel so strongly about these people.

Some individuals find success stories easy to share; in fact, they share them too often! Others are more humble with regard to success. By opening your discussion with their stories of success, you may be able to set a positive stage for the entire conversation. As you jot down the pinnacle of their story, re-celebrate each victorious moment with them.

Keep in mind that your loved ones views of success may be very different from yours. Whether they recall something simple, such as the first time they said grace at dinner, or something more grandiose, like the first time they scored a touchdown, this memory is important to them.

In many large successes, such as graduations, business deals, or community recognition, the reason behind the significance is clear. You may have seen proof of these milestones displayed around your loved one's house in the form of diplomas, plaques, or trophies.

Sometimes, though, the successes that have made the greatest impact on your loved ones are simple moments. Maybe a time when they rescued a small animal or first drove a car. Perhaps the day you were born is the success that stands out to them the most.

Failures, on the other hand, may not be shared so readily or easily. Oftentimes it is difficult to reflect on our failures and put them in context. To have our failures filed away in our memories as "learning experiences" and not "tragic mistakes" is a challenge. Sharing them with someone who wants to record them for posterity can be downright frightening.

Your elder may cringe when recalling a specific memory. After all, you may have put this loved one on a pedestal your whole life, and this conversation could reveal chinks in the armor of your hero. Or perhaps you have had a strained relationship with this person. In that case, you need to accept what he or she shares as simply a piece of who they are and not as an excuse for wrong behavior.

When you're ready to broach this topic, begin by saying that no one is perfect; we have all failed in one way or another. That may help relieve some of the apprehension that admitting failures often carries.

Typically, in retrospect, our failures of the past seem less severe than when they happened. Opening up about them may prove therapeutic.

Some people may chuckle when they recall the circumstances of a particular failure. You may be surprised by either the content of a story or the attitude with which it is expressed. On the other end of the spectrum, there are those who have not come to grips with their failures and might choose not to relate anything. This is their choice. If you have made a sincere offer to listen and accept whatever they have to say, without judgment, you have done all that you can. Perhaps they will open up sometime down the road, after they have had time to consider your query. If not, don't push.

Long before you came to be, your parents probably tried a great many things. Their path to business success may have started with an entrepreneurial lemonade stand or a go-kart that crashed. They may have written a book, played a sport in college, or put together a community service event. Whether these were successes or failures is not important. How they grew through the experience and their willingness to try is the real factor.

No matter what those you care about are willing to offer in this discussion, take whatever is given and use it to understand them better.

Success and Failure

Describe a success in your life:

_____

_____

_____

_____

_____

_____

What did you learn from that experience?

_____

_____

_____

_____

_____

Describe another success in your life:

_____

_____

_____

_____

_____

What did you learn from that experience?

_____

_____

_____

_____

Describe another success in your life:

_____

_____

_____

_____

_____

_____

What did you learn from that experience?

_____

_____

_____

_____

_____

_____

Describe another success in your life:

_____

_____

_____

_____

_____

What did you learn from that experience?

_____

_____

_____

_____

_____

Describe a failure in your life:

_____

_____

_____

_____

_____

What did you learn from that experience?

_____

_____

_____

_____

_____

Describe another failure in your life:

_____

_____

_____

_____

What did you learn from that experience?

_____

_____

_____

_____

_____

Food, Glorious Food

Few things rush memories back to our consciousness as intensely as the smell of food. The aromas that wafted onto our street, front porch, or hallway as we returned home from school or the playground burned an indelible mark on our minds. Tastes of our childhood are brought to the forefront when we smell a favorite meal, baked good, or snack that was cherished in our youth.

We all have our favorites. Meatloaf or pot roast, chicken and biscuits, vegetable soup, or spaghetti. The smell of homemade bread, chocolate cake, or fudge. Some are derived through heritage or ethnicity; others are products of creativity or happenstance.

When we encounter those scents today we may feel instantly whisked away to a time that seemed simpler, when we sat, ate, and enjoyed. Whether we had our meals in a small kitchen, a large dining room, or a living room in front of the TV, the memories can be strong. We pause and bask in this memory and let the world go away, even if for just a short time, as myriad feelings fill our hearts.

Someone important to us worked hard to make those memories, whether knowingly or unwittingly. While we grew, our mothers, fathers or grandparents imprinted themselves on our lives simply by preparing the day's food. They put their hearts into what they made. This was an expression of their love for us.

Some people were taught to cook by a parent, grandparent, or guardian. Others were not so fortunate, especially those who grew up in a more "traditional" time when girls were taught to cook and boys were not. Regardless, just standing next to your favorite cook while he or she made a special dish taught habits and styles.

In the introduction of this book I mentioned a favorite cake that I will never again have because the recipe is locked in the unreachable mind of my mother. Her peanut-butter-fudge frosting was amazing, and I have never found her recipe for it! She also made a fruit salad at Thanksgiving that I had expected to enjoy the rest of my life and pass on to my kids. After all, Mom had a recipe box. But those two recipes aren't there.

Like many good cooks, Mom didn't always follow a page in a book or a card from a box. She picked up shakers of salt, pepper, and other spices and added a pinch here or a dash there. Flour sifted into a bowl, baking powder added, maybe some sugar or cocoa, all done by memory.

If the opportunity still exists for you to capture your flavorful treasures and share them in the future, do not delay. Buy some index cards, make a phone call, and set up a cooking date with your favorite chef. Write down, or let them right down, the recipes as you make the dishes together.

If the recipes you want have been written down already, make copies of them … but still prepare these dishes with your loved ones so you can see the heart of what they do.

Be sure to get the history of each recipe. Who created it? How far back in your family does it go? As your loved ones share memories of the meals they've created, they may feel transported to cherished times of their own. Record their memories along with the recipes.

The following pages have space for cherished recipes and some history notes you may want to make. Please do not let this limited space stop you from gathering as many recipes as you can while you still have the chance.

Special Recipes

Recipe Name:

_____

Shared by:

_____

Created by:

_____

Dated from as far back as:

_____

Historical Notes:

_____

_____

Ingredients:

_____

_____

_____

_____

_____

_____

_____

Directions:

_____

_____

_____

_____

_____

Recipe Name:

_____

Shared by:

_____

Created by:

_____

Dated from as far back as:

_____

Historical Notes:

_____

_____

Ingredients:

_____

_____

_____

_____

_____

_____

Directions:

_____

_____

_____

_____

_____

_____

Recipe Name:

_____

Shared by:

_____

Created by:

_____

Dated from as far back as:

_____

Historical Notes:

_____

_____

Ingredients:

_____

_____

_____

_____

_____

_____

_____

Directions:

_____

_____

_____

_____

_____

_____

Recipe Name:

_____

Shared by:

_____

Created by:

_____

Dated from as far back as:

_____

Historical Notes:

_____

_____

Ingredients:

_____

_____

_____

_____

_____

_____

Directions:

_____

_____

_____

_____

_____

_____

Recipe Name:

_____

Shared by:

_____

Created by:

_____

Dated from as far back as:

_____

Historical Notes:

_____

_____

Ingredients:

_____

_____

_____

_____

_____

_____

Directions:

_____

_____

_____

_____

_____

_____

Joy and Sorrow

Joy and sorrow are powerful ends of the emotional spectrum. Each of us has moments of both in our lives. These points in time have defined much of who we are, whether or not we recognize their effect.

Some people focus primarily on the joyful aspects of their lives. They can regale you with humorous stories of relatives who brought them happiness. They easily share accounts of holidays, birthdays, and ceremonies, that were joyful moments in their lives. Family gatherings, community events, or simple silliness among friends are readily shared.

Other people tend to focus on sorrowful experiences in their past. Perhaps those events happened at a formative time in their lives or they found the circumstances to be overwhelming. The loss of a parent, sibling, or child may stand out vividly because the grief was so intense that it left an open wound, unhealed by time. A traumatic occurrence in their town or the nation might have caused them great sorrow. These incidents may be more difficult for individuals to express to someone else, no matter how close the relationship.

For most people, this discussion will bring out the highs, the lows, and everything in between.

Your elders have had many more years of accumulating these memories than you have. They also have the benefit of hindsight teaching them how to put such memories in the proper context so they can learn from, deal with, and talk about them. While sharing joys and sorrows, your loved ones may feel emotions as intensely as the day the memory happened. Hopefully life has taught them how to pull out those memories, relive the experience, and then file it back to its proper place in their minds.

When your parents, grandparents, or guardians share their joys and sorrows, listen closely. Let them share freely. You might find a memory humorous or absurd, but don't judge. You may see a reflection of yourself in the way their memories are presented and handled.

As with any discussion recommended in this book, take your time and let your loved ones take theirs. If you do, this discussion could become part of the list of joys on your own timeline.

Joys and Sorrows

Describe a joyful time in your past:

_____

_____

How old were you?

_____

What were the circumstances?

_____

_____

_____

_____

_____

_____

_____

_____

_____

_____

_____

_____

_____

_____

_____

_____

Describe another joyful time in your past:

_____

_____

How old were you?

_____

What were the circumstances?

_____

_____

_____

_____

_____

_____

_____

_____

_____

_____

_____

_____

_____

_____

_____

_____

Describe another joyful time in your past:

_____

_____

How old were you?

_____

What were the circumstances?

_____

_____

_____

_____

_____

_____

_____

_____

_____

_____

_____

_____

_____

_____

_____

_____

_____

_____

Describe another joyful time in your past:

_____

_____

How old were you?

_____

What were the circumstances?

_____

_____

_____

_____

_____

_____

_____

_____

_____

_____

_____

_____

_____

_____

_____

_____

Describe a sorrowful time in your life:

_____

_____

_____

How old were you?

_____

What were the circumstances?

_____

_____

_____

_____

_____

_____

_____

_____

How did you cope with it?

_____

_____

_____

_____

_____

_____

_____

_____

_____

_____

Describe another sorrowful time in your life:

_____

_____

_____

How old were you?

_____

What were the circumstances?

_____

_____

_____

_____

_____

_____

_____

_____

How did you cope with it?

_____

_____

_____

_____

_____

_____

_____

_____

_____

Describe another sorrowful moment in your life:

_____

_____

_____

How old were you?

_____

What were the circumstances?

_____

_____

_____

_____

_____

_____

_____

_____

How did you cope with it?

_____

_____

_____

_____

_____

_____

_____

_____

_____

Photos

Most families have lots of photographs. Some are framed and hang on the walls but other loose pictures or organized albums rest in boxes, often gathering dust in a closet or basement. Many are very old, perhaps black-and-white or hued with the natural sepia tones of age. On rare occasions they are pulled out and reminisced over. But in the busyness of life, they tend to be forgotten.

It is quite likely that your elders have a great number of pictures from a time when they had an active life prior to your existence. Snapshots from elementary school, junior high, high school, and college may be the only markers of these events in the timeline of their lives. Family photos with aunts, uncles, and cousins immortalize those relatives on paper for you to enjoy and learn from. Some will likely show faces of people you have never seen or met.

Images of ancestors gathered on porches or in living rooms, around picnic tables or in kitchens, reflect not only who they were but how they lived. Their houses, churches, neighborhoods, or jobs are important links to your heritage. A piece of your lineage rests in these pictures, and you can continue that by passing them on to your children.

A friend of mine recently discovered a box of pictures in his mother's belongings that showed images of his uncle from infancy through high school. Many of the photos included my friend's mom and her sisters.

My friend wanted to show the pictures to his uncle but wasn't sure how receptive he would be to seeing them. So he called to let him know of the discovery. The uncle pondered the thought for a day or two but finally agreed to look at them.

As they pored over the photos, my friend's uncle recalled pets he'd had, houses he lived in, schools he went to, and events in his life that had changed him forever. Reminiscence of his grandparents made him smile. He gave his nephew insights into what their lives were like, and he offered a perspective into my friend's mother that he had never even considered. The experience proved to be a tremendous blessing to both of them.

Carve out time from your busy schedule to make this happen for you and your family. As you open this discussion with your loved ones, keep these things in mind:

1. Be considerate of their feelings. If they decline participation, respect that decision.

2. If they are willing to move forward, give them time to get used to the idea before setting a day and time. Plan it for a week or even a month out.

3. Pick a day when there are no other distractions or commitments.

4. Realize that this may take more than one sitting.

5. You may wish to involve some of your siblings, but if you think that might hinder open, honest conversation, save that for later.

6. Be open to whatever emotional reactions this process might elicit. Traveling this road to the past may bring powerful feelings to the surface in unexpected ways.

7. Let them go at their pace. Don't rush it. Instead of handing them pictures, let them pick the photos up one at a time, show them to you, and share that moment from their past. If they pause in silence before sharing anything about a particular picture, give them time to set themselves in that moment once again.

8. Have paper and pencil ready to jot down what you learn. A lot of information, names, dates, relationships, places, and anecdotal stories will accompany many of the pictures. If you choose to write on the pictures use caution and purchase a proper writing implement so as not to damage the photos.

9. Bring boxes to sort the pictures into categories as you go through them. Afterward, put the photos into albums or folders with your notes included.

When your loved ones pass away or are beyond the capability to relate to these memories, you will have a treasure trove of pictures if you take advantage of the opportunity you have now. And you can pass that treasure on to your own children.

Photos

I've set up a photo-sharing date on this day and time:

_____

At this location:

_____

Who will be present:

_____

_____

_____

_____

Notes:

_____

_____

_____

_____

_____

_____

_____

_____

_____

_____

_____

_____

_____

Notes:

_____

_____

_____

_____

_____

_____

_____

_____

_____

_____

_____

_____

_____

_____

_____

_____

_____

_____

_____

_____

_____

_____

_____

_____

Pitfalls

Life is full of surprises and not all of them are pleasant. The pitfalls your loved ones fell into along the way may vary in intensity from a simple bump in the road to a life-altering turn. These struggles may have come from out of the blue or be the results of decisions they made that had unforeseen effects on their lives.

Some pitfalls might have been recognized and rectified immediately, while others may have taken years to be fully understood and dealt with. For instance, perhaps your loved ones purchased a car or house, not realizing they would be faced with massive, expensive repairs. The issues with the car might have become apparent, and fixed, relatively soon, while the problems with the house might have taken years to overcome.

Some of the obstacles those you care about have faced could be lifelong struggles that remain unresolved. An addiction, for example. No one begins life with the goal of becoming an addict. Yet many find themselves in this or similar traps.

Regardless of the circumstances, the manner in which your loved ones dealt with these situations is critical for you to understand. What one person perceives as a setback another might see as an opportunity.

The goal of this discussion is to find out about the character of those who raised you, because character is built through adversity. If through this discussion you learn from the experience of your elders how to avoid pitfalls in your own life, or at least how to deal with them, that will be an added bonus.

Pitfalls

Describe a pitfall faced:

_____

_____

_____

How old were you?

_____

What were the circumstances?

_____

_____

_____

_____

_____

_____

How did you deal with it?

_____

_____

_____

_____

_____

_____

_____

_____

Describe another pitfall faced:

_____

_____

_____

How old were you?

_____

What were the circumstances?

_____

_____

_____

_____

_____

How did you deal with it?

_____

_____

_____

_____

_____

_____

_____

_____

_____

_____

Recordings

The advent of the phonograph and the movie camera triggered a revolution as to how we store our history. For the first time, people's voices and movements could be captured, not just their still images.

Early on, most of these advancements were reserved for the professional realm of movie makers and radio broadcasters. Public access to these recording devices was limited by such things as wealth and location.

Time and technology marched on, however, making implements of personal imprint readily available. As a result, many people have audio recordings of loved ones singing or chatting. Some families have home movies of birthday parties, snowball fights, or vacations. These nuggets of the past are priceless. Great care should be taken to preserve or restore these treasures.

There are services available that will remaster your old home movies and recordings. If you have any tapes or films sitting in a closet, pull them out and have them processed soon. The longer you wait the more they may degrade.

Once you have them restored, spend an evening viewing them with your family. You will create a new memory just by enjoying those memories together.

While surveying my friends for thoughts on this book, I found several who had no family movies or recordings. They longed to hear Mom's voice or see Dad wave just once more.

Should your elders still be around, you have the power to avoid this tragic loss. Today, most of us have recording devices in our pockets at all times. We pull out our cell phones to check e-mail or text messages. But how often do we take videos of the important people we're with? By making a small effort, you will always be able to hear the voices and see the movements of the people who have enriched your life.

Before you begin to record, make sure everyone grants you permission. Don't record anyone without his or her knowledge and approval. People should be allowed to decline being taped or videoed. Some conversations between family and friends are meant for that setting and those ears only.

Whether you record a conversation or restore home movies, you will be archiving a piece of someone that can be enjoyed forever. By doing this now, you will be able to relive those special moments long after the ones you hold dear have gone.

Recordings of Loved Ones

Event Recorded: _____

Date: _____/_____/_____Type of recording: _____

Where this was recorded:

_____

People present for recording:

_____

_____

Where recording is stored:

_____

Notes:

_____

Event Recorded: _____

Date: _____/_____/_____Type of recording: _____

Where this was recorded:

_____

People present for recording:

_____

_____

Where recording is stored:

_____

Notes:

_____

Event Recorded: _____

Date: _____/_____/_____ Type of recording: _____

Where this was recorded:

_____

People present for recording:

_____

_____

Where recording is stored:

_____

Notes:

_____

_____

Event Recorded: _____

Date: _____/_____/_____ Type of recording: _____

Where this was recorded:

_____

People present for recording:

_____

_____

Where recording is stored:

_____

Notes:

_____

_____

Event Recorded: _____

Date: _____/_____/_____ Type of recording: _____

Where this was recorded:

_____

People present for recording:

_____

_____

Where recording is stored:

_____

Notes:

_____

_____

Event Recorded: _____

Date: _____/_____/_____ Type of recording: _____

Where this was recorded:

_____

People present for recording:

_____

_____

Where recording is stored:

_____

Notes:

_____

_____

Sayings

Many families use sayings, quotations, and cliché's to express themselves. Some of these are teaching tools like "look before you leap." Others could be expletives uttered in times of stress. Regardless of their purpose, these familiar phrases are a part of who your loved ones are.

But where did these sayings come from? Are they derived from ethnic or religious roots? Perhaps they are just the fruit of your loved one's creativity. Might these quotes stem from the colloquial language of the region in which your elder's family settled such as Pennsylvania Dutch or Louisiana Cajun? The line of work that someone labored in might hold clues as to the origin of many quotes that you know so well.

Many individuals seem to quote famous people more often than not. Some tend to mix metaphors, putting a personal and perhaps confusing spin on old sayings.

To illustrate just how much these sayings influence you, consider this: Was there a saying that your parent, guardian, or grandparent used when you were misbehaving as a child that would anger you immensely? Did you ever say, "When I have kids I'm never going to say that to them!" And then when you had children of your own did you hear those same words popping out of your mouth? For many of us this has been the case.

Whether your home was filled with phrases like Ben Franklin's "A penny saved is a penny earned." or some unique saying that no other family has ever heard of, it is enjoyable to log these memories and try to understand their origin. These are, after all, a part of your heritage.

Sayings

Phrase:

_____

Meaning:

_____

Origin:

_____

_____

_____

Phrase:

_____

Meaning:

_____

Origin:

_____

_____

_____

Phrase:

_____

Meaning:

_____

Origin:

_____

_____

_____

Phrase:

_____

Meaning:

_____

Origin:

_____

_____

_____

Phrase:

_____

Meaning:

_____

Origin:

_____

_____

_____

Phrase:

_____

Meaning:

_____

Origin:

_____

_____

_____

Here's to Your Health

Most of us have been to a doctor's office and filled out the questionnaire before our appointment. This form typically asks some questions related to the health of our relatives. Has anyone in your family had cancer? Do any of your relatives have diabetes?

When confronted with these questions, we may find ourselves at a loss for answers. But it is imperative to give our doctors the most complete picture of our health history as possible. They need this tool to properly assess, diagnose, and treat us.

Let's say you see a doctor for a set of symptoms that are common in many diseases or disorders. The doctor performs tests based on those symptoms, testing first for the most common ailments. Through a number of appointments and lab visits, the doctor tries to narrow down the cause of your issue.

All of this takes time, on your part and the doctor's. Tests and procedures are expensive. Your insurance company may deny certain courses of action if they see them as unwarranted given the symptoms you are experiencing and the information your doctor has. Something from your family history may be just the leverage the doctor needs to tip the scales in your favor.

Even conditions that are not inherited can play a significant role in your health. These factors may be related to your environment or to the behaviors of a parent or guardian that has had an effect on you.

Anger, fear, anxiety, addiction, depression and other issues seen in your elders can lead to behaviors in you that might have a profound effect on your physical and mental health. If you accurately relate these influences to your doctors, they will be able to see a complete health history and provide better treatment.

If your parents or guardians have passed on, you may be able to get information you need from an aunt or uncle. If you were adopted, ask the adoption agency if they can provide it.

If you are able to, talk with your loved ones now about family medical history, both physical and mental/emotional. Write down their responses. Then take your notes with you when you have a doctor's appointment so you can convey everything you need to.

Your family's health history may provide rungs to the ladder of your own good health. A conversation with your family members on this topic will also provide significant insight into their past and perhaps even foresight into your future.

Health History

Name of loved one:

_____

Relationship to you:

_____

Write down any health issues experienced (and the year or age when they occurred):

_____

_____

_____

_____

_____

_____

Name of loved one:

_____

Relationship to you:

_____

Write down any health issues experienced (and the year or age when they occurred):

_____

_____

_____

_____

_____

Name of loved one:

_____

Relationship to you:

_____

Write down any health issues experienced (and the year or age when they occurred):

_____

_____

_____

_____

_____

_____

_____

_____

Name of loved one:

_____

Relationship to you:

_____

Write down any health issues experienced (and the year or age when they occurred):

_____

_____

_____

_____

_____

_____

_____

Name of loved one:

_____

Relationship to you:

_____

Write down any health issues experienced (and the year or age when they occurred):

_____

_____

_____

_____

_____

_____

Name of loved one:

_____

Relationship to you:

_____

Write down any health issues experienced (and the year or age when they occurred):

_____

_____

_____

_____

_____

_____

Name of loved one:

_____

Relationship to you:

_____

Write down any health issues experienced (and the year or age when they occurred):

_____

_____

_____

_____

_____

_____

_____

_____

Name of loved one:

_____

Relationship to you:

_____

Write down any health issues experienced (and the year or age when they occurred):

_____

_____

_____

_____

_____

_____

_____

Faith

One of the most difficult aspects of our lives to understand is faith. It is a challenge to give it a specific, succinct definition. Even within a religious denomination or sect, there are differences. If you ask several pastors what faith is, you may get many different answers. When you broach this topic with members of the same congregation, you will often find differences, both subtle and vast, in what faith means to them as individuals.

The same thing is true in families. Your father and mother, even if they came from similar religious backgrounds, might have different views on faith.

Weekly services at a church, temple, or mosque may be family rituals that have formed the basis of their beliefs. Conversely there may have been little or no affiliation with organized religion at all but faith may exist. Even when the same traditions have been practiced and ingrained in the entire family, there are still variations in the interpretation, definition, and subsequent outcome of faith.

Philosophers and theologians have discussed, debated, argued, and postulated faith-related questions for millennia. Is there a God? If so, what is he (or she) like? What does God want us to do? Where do we go when we die? How do I believe in something I cannot see? Or can I see God but am just not looking for the right thing?

These questions cannot be answered within these pages. However, if you ask your loved ones for their thoughts, the responses will enlighten you as to their faith.

Asking "What do you believe?" seems simple right? But the answers you get may surprise you.

You may get a response that has been ingrained by repetition. Or the question may elicit a rapid "I believe ..." followed by a long pause as the person grasps for an answer. Perhaps your elder will offer a deep, rich explanation of their faith.

Answering "Why do you believe that?" may be more difficult. Your loved ones might become defensive, as if they are trying to justify what they believe. They might not know why they believe. On the other hand, some people may relate a spiritual experience that substantiates their faith.

Whatever answers you get to these questions, remember that your loved ones have every right to their own beliefs and feelings without condemnation. So as you prepare to approach someone on this topic, keep these things in mind:

1   Be sure your motive is not to change the other person's beliefs to match your own. Make it clear that you are only trying to understand them better. Do whatever you can to make them feel safe in the conversation.

2   Be prepared to hear the unexpected. If you go into this conversation with preconceived notions about what the other person believes, you may close this door of understanding forever. Even a surprised expression on your face may shut them down, creating a guarded, contrived response that merely tells you what he or she thinks you want to hear.

3   Listen more than you speak. Once you have opened the door, let them take control of the conversation. If there is something you don't understand, ask for clarification. But do so in a manner that is not threatening or condemning.

4   Enjoy this time with your loved one. There is an intimacy to faith that does not exist in many other topics. You may be seeing a raw part of the soul that few, if any, have ever seen.

5   Allow this conversation to spread into more than one sitting. You may not get full answers to your questions right away simply because the individual has not truly considered them. Oftentimes people have trouble expressing what they believe in words. This discussion may open up a lifelong conversation as your loved one ponders how to explain his or her faith to you.

Start this conversation as soon as you can. The more time your loved ones have to consider their answers, and the more time you have to process them together, the richer your relationship with them will be. For the rest of your life you will carry a piece of them in your heart that cannot be obtained after they have passed away.

What about Faith?

What do you believe about God and faith?

_____

_____

_____

_____

_____

_____

_____

Why do you believe these things?

_____

_____

_____

_____

_____

_____

_____

_____

_____

_____

_____

_____

_____

End-of-Life Wishes

Of all the conversations suggested in this book, end-of-life wishes may be the most avoided. It is, however, a topic that should be addressed with a degree of urgency in order to ensure that your loved one's desires are honored.

By taking the time to broach this subject, you are being proactive in protecting the rights of the ones you love. If you have the their requests in writing, there can be no doubt as to the steps that should be taken with regards to emergency health care, a memorial after passing on, and the distribution of possessions.

Throughout the process of discerning your loved ones end-of-life wishes, they will be making many decisions. They will choose a health-care proxy, someone who makes medical decision on their behalf should they become incapacitated. A power of attorney might be assigned in order to handle their legal affairs. The appointment of an executor to take care of estate distribution is important. These responsibilities might fall to one person or they may be spread over several people.

Keep in mind, they might not choose you for these tasks. After all, they may be protecting you from making difficult decisions in a stressful time.

How these end-of-life issues are handled from a legal standpoint varies from state to state. It is always beneficial to seek local legal counsel to ensure accurate and binding documentation for your jurisdiction. Senior Citizen or End-of-Life advocacy groups may exist in your area to provide guidance. There are many websites that can provide some direction on this topic as well.

Should your loved ones balk at this process, your options are limited. It is, once again, their choice. However, they may soften to the idea just by considering your suggestion to create a plan.

The passing of those we care about is a stressful time. Families have found themselves divided when faced with life-or-death decisions of those they love. Who gets what or how much can create rifts in relationships that can span a lifetime. If there is a solid end-of-life plan in place, many of those relationships can be saved and enjoyed.

Provided is a checklist of some suggested steps to have in place for end-of-life issues. Feel free to add or subtract from this list as your situation dictates.

End-of-Life Wishes Checklist

o   Advanced Health Care Directive
    (How you want to be treated at the end of your life)

o   Living Will
    (Details the type of medical life-support treatment you do or do not want at the end
    of your life)

o   Health Care Proxy
    (Designated person to advocate for you in healthcare decisions when you cannot)

o   Pre-paid Funeral Arrangements
    (Available at many funeral homes)

o   Memorial/Funeral Service

o   Burial/Cremation

o   Last Will and Testament
    (Legal document that depicts a person's final wishes in regards to dependents and
    possessions)

o   Executor
    (Designated person to carry out the terms of the last will and testament)

o   Power of Attorney
    (Person designated in writing to act on your behalf in legal matters)

o   Joint bank accounts established with Power of Attorney

Give the Recipe Now

Most of this book has been devoted to obtaining information about those who have led you through your life. But those who follow you deserve the same things you seek. There will come a time when your children will wonder about these topics with regard to your history. The only one who can give them the answers is you.

You have the recipes for the foods your children remember and cherish. Filed inside you are anecdotes of family history, stories that bring to life not just who you are but who your parents and the rest of your relatives were. You may have a box in the closet filled with family photos, movies, or videos. The hobbies you had as a child, or the hopes and dreams you entertained, could be guiding forces that led your offspring onto the paths they walk. The faith you share with them might be the foundation they cling to in times of trial and are grateful for in times of joy.

Letting the next generation know how you've handled success, failure, joy, and sorrow could enable them to celebrate or endure those things in a way that will enhance their lives. They may be able to sidestep pitfalls that you fell into if you give them the warning signs. Should your kids fall into the same traps, they might find comfort in knowing that you recovered from them yourself.

Write down everything you can think of, preferably in your own handwriting. Share every recipe, anecdote, success, and failure. Get those old movies and recordings copied. Make new recordings and video yourself speaking to your children. Let them hear your voice ... and your faith.

This is the most powerful gift you can ever give. The definition of your legacy. A complete recipe of who you are.

What Will I Give?

Jot down notes as you consider what you will give to those who follow you:

_____

_____

_____

_____

_____

_____

_____

_____

_____

_____

_____

_____

_____

_____

_____

_____

_____

_____

_____

_____

_____

_____

_____

Finally

Through our lives we make statements like "I don't have time for this" and "I need to make time for that." But we cannot *make* time. We all have the same twenty-four hours a day, and none of us knows how many days we will have. All we can do is decide what we will do with the time we are given.

As you follow the steps in this book, taking the time to get the questions you want answered by your loved ones, live life with them. Cook with them, write to them, look at pictures with them, laugh with them, and love them while you still can.

Extra Notes and Scrapbook

These pages are provided for any notes you feel are important to the recipe of who your loved one is or for any scraps from the past that you might wish to store.

_____

_____

_____

_____

_____

_____

_____

_____

_____

_____

_____

_____

_____

_____

_____

_____

_____

_____

_____

_____

_____
_____
_____
_____
_____
_____
_____
_____
_____
_____
_____
_____
_____
_____
_____
_____
_____
_____
_____
_____
_____
_____
_____
_____
_____
_____
_____
_____
_____
_____

www.ingramcontent.com/pod-product-compliance
Lightning Source LLC
Chambersburg PA
CBHW081657270326
41933CB00017B/3197